Memories
of
St Ninians

Willie Jenkins

Stirling Council **Libraries**
Community Services

Published by

 **Libraries**
Community Services

Library Headquarters
Borrowmeadow Road
Springkerse Industrial Estate
Stirling FK7 7TN
Tel. 01786 432383
Fax. 01786 432395

ISBN 1 870 542 39 8

Printed by
Cordfall Ltd Glasgow
0141 572 0878

FOREWORD

The ancient parish of St Ninians, which surrounded Stirling is at the centre of Scotland's history. Its old name of Eccles and its present name of St Ninians show its roots in the Celtic Church; Robert the Bruce and Bonnie Prince Charlie both left their imprint on the area.

The village of St Ninians was the largest settlement and now runs without a break into Stirling. However there are many who look on the community of St Ninians as more than just a suburb of its larger neighbour.

This book of photographs, enthusiastically compiled by Willie Jenkins, celebrates St Ninians' individuality and the lives of its people at work and leisure.

Willie Jenkins is one of the 'characters' of St Ninians. There can have been little happening this century which he does not know about at first hand, or at most second hand. His encyclopaedic knowledge of the village, his tireless enthusiasm for collecting old photographs, his capacity for endless hard work in gleaning information, his willingness to share his knowledge with others through talks or the printed word, all led deservedly to his being awarded 'The Provost's Prize' in 1998. This book is one way of passing his knowledge on to future residents of St Ninians.

Although every effort has been made to trace copyright holders of all the photographic material used in this book, inevitably one or two may have slipped through the net. If this is the case, apologies are made in advance.

ACKNOWLEDGEMENTS

Whyler (Photographers), Hamish and Jim Mailer; Jim Mather; Mrs Lucy Thomson; Gilbert Ferguson; Mrs Jenny Ross; Jim Ormiston; Mrs Rosanna Tortolano; Willie Nugent; Mrs Robert Vallance; Jimmy Wilson; David McInnes; Mrs Mary Bell; David Stirling; Mrs Ina Rutherford; Willie Erskine; Julian Lindsay; Mrs Mary Jenkins; Stirling Council Archives Services; Smith Art Gallery and Museum

A special thanks to John Norrie for his contribution of original postcards towards this publication, and to Annabel Griffin for her typing skills.

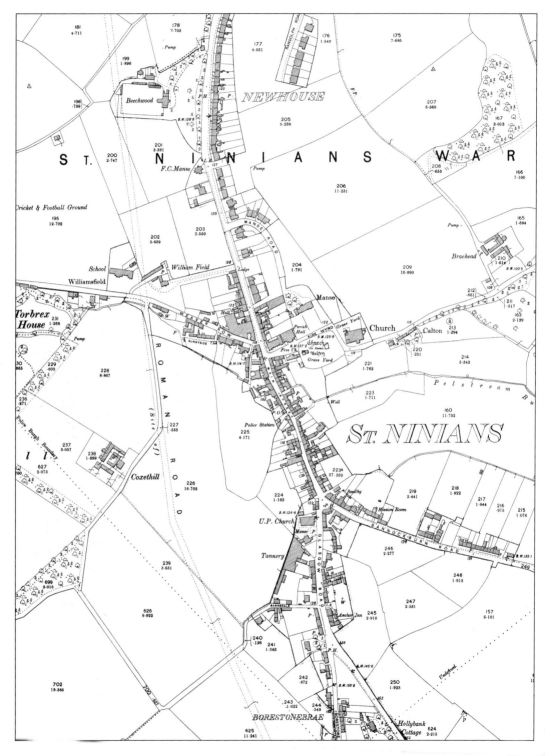

1996 Map produced by Harvey Maps and Stirling Council.

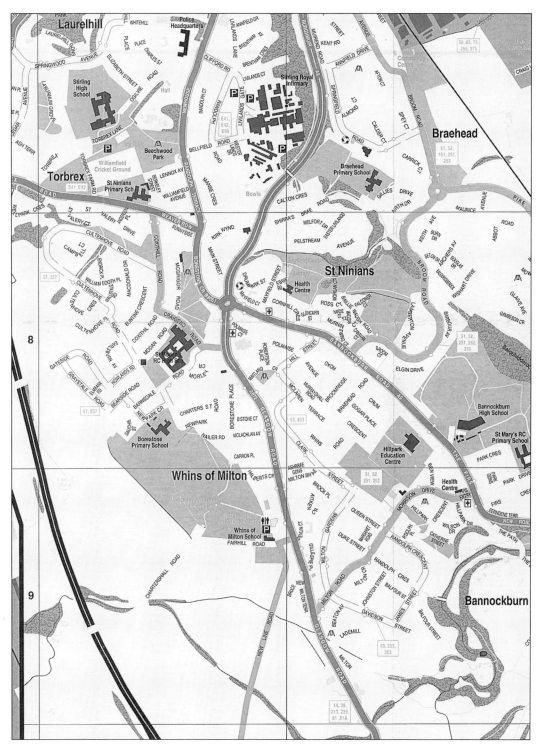

© Harvey Maps reproduced with permission.

The photograph on the end pages was taken from what is now McGrigor Road, the site of Holy Spirit Church, one of Stirling's four Roman Catholic Churches. It opened for worship on Sunday 20th December 1964, its first priest being the Very Reverend Canon Patrick Rourke. Canon Rourke retired in September 1998 after thirty four years' service to the Church, and a special Mass of thanksgiving was held to thank Canon Rourke and to welcome the new priest, Father Alex Bremner.

Nailmaking has been associated with St Ninians since the late eighteenth century, when the trade gave employment to over 100 individuals, many of whom were young boys. By the 1850s, machinery had reduced much of the drudgery, although a hand nailer still worked in St Ninians as recently as the 1950s.

On the left of this photograph is part of J. & W. Sommerville Ltd's Nailworks. The local bus is negotiating 'Nailworks Corner', at that point only about twenty feet wide. During 1930-31 the firm demolished part of its premises and rebuilt further back, to allow the Town Council to widen the road.

This resulted in a dramatic improvement, shown in this post-card produced in the early 1930s for A. J. Clark, who ran the St Ninians Post Office. The nailworks (on left) moved to Lennoxtown in 1940, and a supermarket chain now occupies the site.

On the opposite side of the road are, left to right, a chip shop, the 'Scots Wha Ha'e' public house, Mr Clark's Post Office (which incorporated a lending library), a fruiterer, and a sweet shop.

Inside the workshops of James Brown and Sons, nailmakers and foundry furnishers, Sunnyside, Weaver Row, St Ninians, c.1936/38.

Left to Right: David Irons Brown; Nettie Rennie; John Gibb; John Brown (brother of David); William Valentine.

Another industry long associated with St Ninians was bolt making. Thomas Brown's firm of nailworks and bolt manufacturers was well established by 1868. After his death in 1893 the firm passed to his family, and it moved to new premises in Sunnyside, Weaver Row in 1908 from where it operated until its closure in 1964.

Thomas Brown and his wife Janet Wright.

Although in 1845 the parish of St Ninians could boast 19 schools the 'Statistical Account' of that year noted that while 'most parents are zealous for the education of their children, a spirit of indifference is certainly increasing'. School fees were beyond the purses of most families, who tended to send their children out to work as soon as possible, to contribute to the family income. By 1868 there were two schools in St Ninians itself, a United Presbyterian school and St Ninians Parish School. William Knox L.L.D. was school master here, a post he held with that of 'inspector of poor and collector of rates, registrar of births, marriages and deaths, and session-clerk.'

St Ninians Public School opened in Weaver Row on 11th May 1876. This first photograph shows the entire school assembled in the hall decorated to celebrate the Coronation of King George V in 1911, the other is a typical example of an individual class group with their teacher.

Football has long been part of school life, from the informal 'keepie-uppie' of the playground to the more formal team games. St Ninians Public School football team of 1929 was trained by Jimmy Bryans (left) seen in this group with Alexander Menzies (right) the recently-appointed headmaster.

Of the aspiring McCoists or Gazzas, only one in this photograph is known, Joe France (second left, back row) youngest son of Abraham and Mary France, owners of the Borestone Cafe in Borestone Crescent.

St Ninians Public School
Weaver Row
Class of 1943 - 44

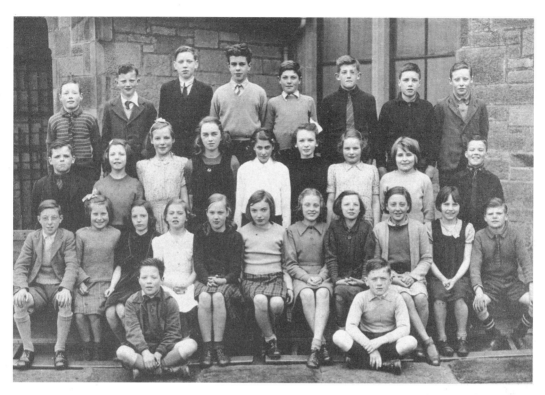

Left to right

Back row: J McRae; Kenny Smith; Billy Boyd; Ian Brisbane; John Young;
      Freddy France, Wull Dick, Jim McRorie.

Middle row: David "Spooky" Miller; Betty Paton; Cathie Shanks; Doreen Neville;
      Jean Bruce; Margaret Crawford; Violet Still; Anne Simpson; Willie Limond.

Front row: Jimmy Anderson; Mary Currie; Jean Martin; Helen Mitchell; Betty Todd;
      Davina Murphy; Edith Gillies; Ada McKenzie; Agnes Malcolmson; Betty Hannigan;
      Alex Thomson.

Sitting in front: John McAllister; John Nugent.

Returning to Main Street from our detour to Sunnyside, this photograph shows the view from 'Nailworks Corner' towards Stirling. Although the buildings on the right are still standing, albeit much changed, those on the left were demolished to make way for Caledonia Place, built in 1903, and for Randolph Buildings built in 1911.

In the centre is one of the fleet of tramcars which linked St Ninians with Stirling and Bridge of Allan. The first horse-drawn car set off to St Ninians in January 1898, a petrol-driven rival appearing just before World War I.

Both continued to run for some years after the War, but public preference for the new motor bus eventually defeated them, and the tramcar services came to an end in 1920.

The trees on the left of the previous photograph mark the entrance to Williamfield House, built in 1682 by William Wordie for his wife Jean Milne. It remained in the Wordie family for three more generations but by 1823 it was owned by James Chrystal, a lawyer. Since then various parts of the property have been sold off. Firstly, in 1875, the School Board bought an acre as a site for a public school, then in 1909 it was bought by James and William Ronald, a firm of builders who were responsible for Lennox Avenue, Berkeley Street and Williamfield Avenue. The house is still in private ownership, Stirling Council Cricket Club owning the remaining land.

Still at 'Nailworks Corner', but this time looking south down Main Street where, on the left, part of St George's Church can just be seen. Beyond the group of people round the lamp-post is no. 31, a house and shop owned at the time the photograph was taken by John Johnstone, an antique dealer whose family owned the property for almost a century. This house was also built by a William Wordie in 1629, and entry to it was by Parliament Arch, 1 Kirk Wynd.

On the right, at 44 Main Street, is Mrs Glen's Family Grocery business, taken over in 1913 by a former St Ninian's resident, Mr Chrystal. On April 25th 1903, Borestone Crescent was opened, running from alongside Mrs Glen's property to the Toll.

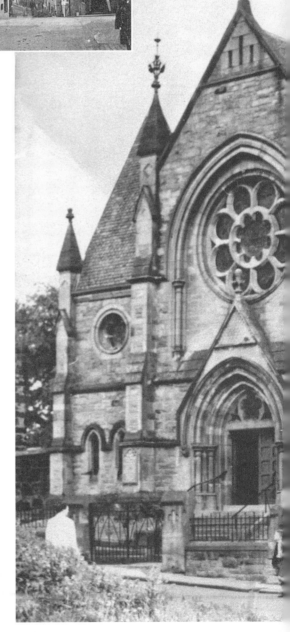

St George's Church, in Main Street and Kirk Wynd, was opened for worship on Thursday 11th June 1885 by Dr Bonnar of Glasgow. It was originally St Ninians Free Church but took the name of St George's in 1929 after the union of the two churches. In 1968, after having been without a minister for two years, following the retiral of the Reverend George Martin in 1966, it was decided to dissolve the charge, and the final service was held on Sunday 15th December 1968. The building was demolished between 1973-74 and a new housing complex was built on the site by the council with tenants moving in during October 1978.

An interior view of St George's in 1960, when the church was decorated for Christmas. The 1885 building took the place of an earlier and smaller church, now the Parish Halls, which was opened on Sunday 24th September 1843.

This cheerful group was photographed outside St George's Church about 1959. The Reverend George Martin, who ministered at St George's from 1956 until 1966, is in the centre and Brownie Leader Mrs Hunter is on the right of the group.

This modern photograph of St Ninians Old Parish Church was taken from the steeple by a steeplejack whilst making repairs to the lightning conductor. In the foreground can be seen the ruins of the church which was blown up by Prince Charles' troops on February 1, 1746. The inner relief road, seen here on the right, was opened in July 1964 thus making Kirk Wynd a cul-de-sac to through traffic, and also denying pedestrians access to Shirra's Brae. Thus a pedestrian walk-way was constructed, the entrance to which is visible near the bus to the right.

Interior of the Old Parish Church built in 1750.

This photograph was taken about 1920 at Calton, Shirra's Brae, the home of Mrs Jean Wilson who can be seen 3rd on the left. The others in the photograph are from left: Colin Rae; Mrs Rae; Mrs Wilson; and sitting on the chair William Donaldson, Mrs Wilson's brother. This cottage, one of three, has now been modernised and is occupied by Mr and Mrs Charles Edie.

This fine view is the front of Easter Livilands House, Shirra's Brae which in 1930, when this photograph was taken, was owned by Mr Archibald Holme Mowbray who had purchased it in 1926. In 1962-63 the house building firm Mowlem Ltd purchased the estate and proceeded to build private housing on what is now Pelstream Avenue and Melfort Drive. By 1967 the mansion house itself had been so badly vandalised it had to be demolished and in 1970 more housing was built.

Main Street about 1934

Looking north towards the nailworks where the Somerfield Store now stands, the ruined building on the left was the mansion house built for Robert Rollo of Powhouse. This building was known as the Gallery and was built between 1670 and 1680. Robert Rollo was one of four overseers appointed to conduct the first election of Stirling Town Council in 1689. Some of the houses on the right were empty by 1934, the tenants having moved to new council housing in the Raploch and Drip Road area of Stirling.

Returning to Main Street this first view looks south from Nailworks Corner. The first building on the left with the thatched roof is dated 1629 and at the time of this picture was used as an antique shop run by Mr Johnstone who lived above the shop. In 1932 when his daughters were running the business a firework set the roof on fire, destroying the thatch which was then replaced by slates. The building was taken over by the Town Council and was the only building left when the redevelopment took place. It was made into two flats by 1976.

Mr Johnstone's neighbour at no. 33 was James Lawrie also known as Sanny who ran a cycle shop. His workshop and store were at no. 37 where there were the three residences of J. McCormack, J. Campbell and L. Walker. In between at no. 35 was Mr J. Mann, while no. 39 was the home of Mrs C. Ure. To the right of the photograph where the children are standing is no. 64 Main Street with the respective homes of R. Smith, J. Tarlton, W. Graham, J. Morrison, Mrs C. Valentine, A. Shaw and J. Orr. No. 66 was the home of Mrs Ann Muirhead, whose neighbour at no. 68 was George Smith. Beside the lamp post is no. 70 of which only the attic is shown. This was the home of R. Dick, but other occupiers of the building were W. Caddies and J. McDonald. Miss Mary Keenan, affectionately known as 'Auld Cook', had a house and shop at no. 72.

A narrow path between nos 72 and 76 gave access to no. 74 where the homes of T. Morton, Mrs J. Laird, A. Cameron, N. Bonnar, A. Orr, J. Lambie and S. Cattigan could be found. W. Orr, T. McQuillan, D. Malcomson and A. Martin all had homes at no. 76. John Cullen lived at no. 78 while at no. 80 were the homes of J. Nugent, W. Brown, Mrs Ann Gemmell and N. McDiarmid. David Jenkins, greengrocer, known as 'Tatty Davy' occupied no. 82 and also had a stable for his horse and cart here. Miss Edith Baxter lived at no. 84 while no. 86 was Mr James Duffy's grocery shop. One of the houses at no. 88 was empty while the other was occupied by Frederick Murdoch.

Old Main Street, St. Ninians, Stirling

Brucefield Dairy at no. 83 Main Street was occupied for many years by Malcolm McLaren. Milk was collected from the farms and delivered fresh daily to customers by horse and cart. Above the dairy lived Mr and Mrs William Goodwin and above them to the left of the blocked-up window was Mrs Boyd with Mrs Murray on the right. Between the Dairy and the Grosvenor Cafe is the close leading to McDiarmid's Candleworks. Access to the houses above the shops was also through the close. These were occupied by Pietre Janetta, James Murray, Mrs E. Boyd, James Penman and William Goodwin. Pietre Janetta's stable was also through the close. Pietre Janetta ran the Grosvenor Cafe as a chip shop and ice cream parlour. To the right of the Grosvenor Cafe was Mr William Dunn's shop.

Opposite:
Three examples of Mr Janetta's delivery vans.

Still looking north from St Ninian's Toll the properties in 1931 were occupied by on the left, no. 146, Tavern and public house owned and occupied by Miss Barbara Burnett. The houses above the shops at nos. 142 and 140 were owned by Stirling Co-operative Society and were lived in by, at 142 R. Taylor, Peter Simpson, A. Wright, Frank Smith, Mrs Mary Anne Gair and T. Bingham, at no. 140 by Peter Hay, J Murray, A. Cunningham and Mrs Anne Watt. No. 140 was also the Co-op butcher's shop with the grocery department next door at no. 138. Alex Kerr lived at no. 136, while his neighbour was Mr William Martin Jr who lived at no. 134. No. 130 was the store used to ripen bananas by Robert Machray, fruit merchant and the shop at no. 128 was that of Scott Brothers, plumbers. Above this were the houses of no. 126 occupied by Mrs Mary Ann Scott, John Scott, plumber, William Muir and A. Menzies. No. 126 (not shown in photograph) was the bakehouse and store belonging to Kerr and Wallace, bakers. In the middle of the picture can be seen the gable end window of fruit merchant Mr John Jenkins' house. John Simpson's butcher's shop was at no. 122 with a Mrs Simpson living in the house above. At no. 118 were the homes of Mrs Simpson, George Paterson, William Bryans and Robert Bryans, with Mrs Paul Morton living at no. 114.

Across the road in the right foreground at no. 97 was Alexander Lamond and Sons' saddlers business. C. Mitchell, David Bateman, and John Hughes lived respectively at nos. 95, 93 and 91. William Dunn occupied the house and shop at no. 89.

W. Mitchell, baker occupied the shop and tea-room at 3 Bannockburn Road, at St Ninians Toll. The bakehouse and store were at 99, Main Street.

At 1 Bannockburn Road were the two houses occupied by Archibald Young and by Agnes Crawford, while at no. 5 lived William Mitchell. The two houses at no. 7 were occupied by A. McNaughton and by Catherine McGregor. Mitchell and Sons' stables and garage were also at no. 7.

St Ninian's Toll was known locally as St Ringans Toll. J. Walls' blacksmiths shop can be seen on the left above which were the houses lived in by David Dickson, David Paterson, Mrs Elizabeth Nimmo and Andrew Ewing. Margaret Ewing and Isabella McDonald lived at nos 13 and 15 respectively. In the centre of the photograph is the old Borestone Bar run by Mrs Mary Brimer. This was demolished around 1936 to allow the Town Council to widen the Bannockburn and Glasgow Roads. The new Borestone Bar was built in 1937. Part of the United Free South Church can be seen to the right of the old Borestone Bar.

In this photograph can be seen the new Borestone Bar, with the roundabout under construction. Full licence was granted to owner/occupier Harry Brimer in October 1937.

Beyond Miss Barbara Burnett's Tavern is no. 150 Main Street, three houses occupied by G. McCallum, R. Thorburn and S. Dixon. No.152 was occupied by George McNaughton while at no.154, the last house on this side of the street lived, James McDonald.

The St Ninians United Free South Church situated at St Ninians Toll was built as a Relief Church in 1774. The last service was held in 1934 and the building was used as a garage store until it was demolished around 1969.

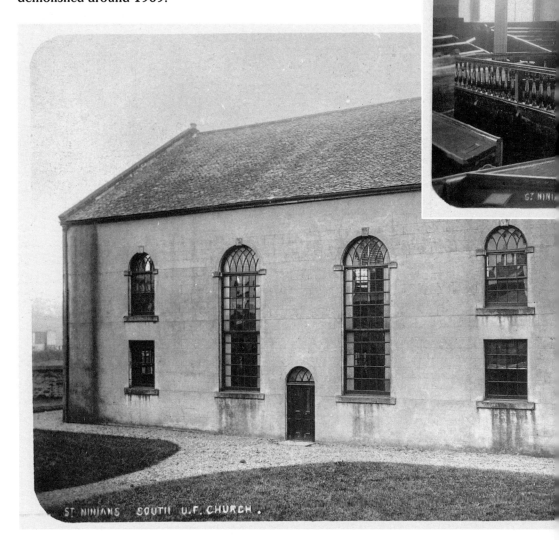

ST NINIANS SOUTH U.F. CHURCH.

CHURCH   INTERIOR

The longest serving Minister was the Reverend Robert Frew who served the congregation for 75 years from 1835-1910. The interior view is taken from a postcard produced by Mark Bennett, a well known photographer in St Ninians. His work is easily recognised by the curved corners and his practice of labelling each image in white ink.

This view of St Ninians Toll shows, on the left, part of the United Free Manse with the garage and filling station owned by Abe France next door. On the right of the photograph can be seen the gable end of no. 154 Main Street with the telephone box in front of it. The outside wash house can also be seen and to the left of this is the Borestone Cafe owned by Abe France. There was also a billiard room here and two houses above the cafe.

This photograph was taken at Abe France's garage in Borestone Crescent. Featured in the photograph with visiting relatives and two mechanics are from left to right Mary France; Joe France; Will Cook and Margaret Cook.

Borestone Park was the home ground of St Ninians Thistle Football Club (also known as 'The Jags'), from 1905 until it was disbanded in 1940. The Club was formed in 1897, playing in the Junior League. Although plans for a grandstand were passed by the Council in 1900, it was never built.

Pictured sixth from the left, back row, the goalkeeper Bob Aitken, a slaterer from Main Street, was capped for Scotland in the Junior Association Match against Ireland in 1908.

This photograph shows St Ninians Thistle Football Club who were winners of the Victory League Club and the Stirlingshire Cup in the season 1933-34.

In the back row from left to right are J. Kaninsky; W. Martin; A. Ure; A. Forsyth; J. Neil and G. McCallum.

In the front row from left to right are J. Ross; T. Milroy; R. Richardson; R. Withers and D. McInnes.

This charming group in front of the Borestone Cafe at 55 Borestone Crescent shows Mr Abraham (known as Abe or Aby) France, his wife Mary holding their baby, and to the far left, their daughter Jenny. The identity of the two young lads dressed up in their kilts is unknown. The family lived above the shop before building a bungalow next to the billiard room. The petrol filling station, garage and adjoining hut were opened by Mr France across the road from the cafe. These were looked after by his son Freddy, and a filling station still operates from these premises.

Opposite:
The hut was used as the venue for Burns Suppers run by St Ringans Burns Club. Here we see (from left to right) Wull Cross; Wull Cook; Jim McDonald and Agnes Crawford, suitably attired for just such an occasion.

Looking north down Main Street, St Ninians Toll has been decorated to celebrate the Coronation of King Edward VII on June 26th 1902.

The white cottages on the left attached to the St Ninians Tavern were demolished to allow the Stirling Co-op to erect a three storey building (including two shops, butcher's and grocer's) and flats.

The shops and houses continued to be occupied until the late 1960s when they were demolished during the new development of Main Street.

The Co-op moved into new premises during 1968 as part of the new shopping precinct built in Bannockburn Road, St Ninians.

A group of locals is pictured at St Ninians Toll, dressed up for the annual Charity Parade which was held for several years to raise funds for Stirling Royal Infirmary. This photograph was taken around 1943, and the houses of Bannockburn Road can be seen in the background.

In the group are (left to right): May Beattie; unknown; Jimmy Mather; Jean Mains; Bob Starkey, well known as a heavyweight competitor at Highland Games; Netta Millar; the last three figures are unidentified.

This is the Glasgow Road looking south from St Ninians. All the houses, shops and cottages on the right-hand side were demolished from the Toll up to the foot of the Borestone Brae during the late 1960s. This was to allow a dual carriageway to be constructed along with modern housing on the site.

Opposite:
Charles Machray established his motor hirer's business at Braeside Garage, Glasgow Road, in 1899. The first of these two photographs shows a group of Machray's taxi drivers at the taxi rank, Station Road, Stirling, left to right George Murray; unknown; John Machray; Robert White; unknown. In the second, a group of Charles Machray's employees and friends pose outside Braeside Garage before leaving on an annual outing.

Pictured around 1930 outside the smiddy beside Laburnum Cottage, now 80 Glasgow Road, Whins of Milton, St Ninians are, from left to right: John McLachlan; James Squair; Robert Leighton; William Dick; Mr Paton; John Struthers; Alex Murdoch; John Pollock; John Leighton; J. Crawford. Some of these men had small smiddies in St Ninians and were employed by John McLachlan who supplied the steel for this purpose. Most of the men were sons of the early nailers who worked in St Ninians. Mr John McLachlan had been asked by a newspaper representative if he would allow some of his employees to pose for this photograph. John McLachlan had taken over the business founded about 1841 by his father Archibald McLachlan who built Laburnum Cottage.

James Squair was one of the last hand-nailers in St Ninians. He lived in Bannockburn, and had been blacksmith at nearby Auchenbowie Estate. He worked for Mr McLachlan from about 1928 until 1938, when he joined the firm of J and W Somerville, and moved with them to Lennoxtown in 1940.

These workers were known as nailers, but at the time this photograph was taken in 1938, they made pipe tools and gutter hooks for the building industry. William Erskine, grandson of Archibald McLachlan who started the hand nail industry served most of his time in India after being called up to the Army. When he was demobbed, he started a small business making the same articles at a small foundry in Dunipace. Back row (left to right): William Erskine; unknown; James Edmond. Front row (left to right): James Squair; James Tough; David Forshaw.

Off the Glasgow Road in Borestone Place is St Ninians United Free Church.

The first picture shows the congregation outside the church on 5 April 1981 after they celebrated 50 years as a reformed congregation.

The second photograph shows the congregation on 21 October 1994 after a special thanksgiving service inside the church marking 60 years of worship in that building.

Traditionally the site where Robert the Bruce raised his standard at the Battle of Bannockburn in 1314, the Borestone itself suffered from souvenir hunters to such an extent that a protective grill was put in place over it in 1836. The original outcrop is now under concrete. The site itself has been developed by the National Trust for Scotland as a visitor centre. The flagstaff was erected in 1870 by the Dumbarton Lodge of Ancient Order of Independent Oddfellows with the Stirling Rock of Hope Lodge paying for the foundations. The visitor shelter was erected around 1894. The bronze statue of Robert the Bruce was designed by C d'O Pilkington Jackson and was unveiled by H. M. The Queen on 24 June 1964, the 650th anniversary of Bruce's great victory, after she had opened the nearby Rotunda.

The Borestone Bowling Club was situated at the foot of Brocks Brae, near the flagpole. This picture, taken around 1870 shows the bowlhouse which was demolished in 1892 and replaced with a small brick clubhouse which in turn was demolished in 1955. Its replacement, opened in 1956, was extended in the 1970s and is still in use.

The Club won the Stirling County Bowling Association McKillop Trophy in 1896. After winning it again in 1898 and 1902 they were given permanent possession of the trophy and it was used up until the 1970s as the Green Championship Trophy.

The identity of one of the bowlers is known – the gentleman on the seat on the extreme left is George Jenkins. Each member of the trophy winning team was gifted with a gold medal, and Mr Jenkins' medal is still with the family.

Borestone bowlers with trophy.

Chartershall hamlet was once a community of nailmakers. Situated west of Whins of Milton beside the Bannock Burn, it consisted mainly of small cottages and the smiddies for the hand-nail makers. There was also a small parish school. A wooden bridge, built over the Bannock Burn in 1610, was replaced by a stone bridge in 1720. With the opening of the M9 Motorway which runs adjacent to Chartershall a new road bridge had to be built. The hamlet now consists of a few cottages, some council houses and one or two newly built houses.

Chartershall House was built as a convalescent home for Stirling Royal Infirmary in 1906 and opened by the Duchess of Montrose on 28 July of that year. Because of its inaccessibility by bus, and the fact that it was too small to permit the development of a true community spirit, it was given up. The property has now been divided into two private houses.

This group photograph was taken at Livilands Bowling Green in May 1922, at the opening of the green for the new season.

Livilands Bowling Club was formed in 1910 and the green opened at Livilands Gate on 14th July 1910. With the hospital board purchasing the green and premises, the club played its final game on the old green during August 1975.

On Saturday 1st May 1976 the club opened its new green and clubhouse at Randolph Road. The opening ceremony was performed by Mrs MacReadie, wife of the Chairman of the Forth Valley Health Board.

Left to right: Mr MacReadie; J. D. Kennedy, CBE; Club President; Mrs MacReadie; and Mr Tom Walls, Vice President.

Newhouse marks the unofficial boundary between Stirling and St Ninians. The tramlines used by the Stirling/St Ninians tramcars can be seen.

Most of the houses on the right hand side of the Stirling/St Ninians Road were demolished and a new housing complex in a cul-de-sac was erected, tenants moving in about October 1964.

Opposite is the estate of Beechwood which has been used for a number of years by the Town Council as offices, and at present Bett, housebuilders, propose to develop the site for private housing.

The landmark of the outside stair on to the pavement at Newhouse disppeared about 1904 when the owner of the property had the building demolished. This was replaced by a new building of four flats all at no. 2 Newhouse during 1905.

Randolphfield Police Headquarters is situated behind the hedge on the extreme right. The names Randolphfield and Clifford Road commemorate the skirmish between the infantry of Randolph and the cavalry of Clifford prior to the Battle of Bannockburn.

FURTHER READING

BODEY, HUGH *Nailmaking*.
　　[Shire Publications Ltd. Aylesbury] **1983**

FLEMING, J.S. *Ancient Castles and Mansions of Stirling Nobility*.
　　[Paisley and London] **1902**

GROOM, FRANCIS *Ordnance Gazeteer of Scotland*.
　　[London, Edinburgh, Glasgow] N/D

MCCUTCHEON, R. AND B. *Pictures from the Past – first series*.
　　[Stirling] **1984**

MCCUTCHEON, R. AND B. *Pictures from the Past: Stirling's 'Neebour' Villages*.
　　[Stirling] **1985**

MCKEAN, CHARLES *Stirling and the Trossachs*.
　　[Edinburgh] **1985**

MAIR, CRAIG *Stirling the Royal Burgh*.
　　[John Donald Publishers Ltd in Association with Stirling District Libraries,
　　Edinburgh] **1995**

PAGET-TOMLINSON, EDWARD *The Railway Carriers*.
　　[Lavenham] **1990**

The Royal Commission on the Ancient and historical Monuments of Scotland
　　Stirlingshire, an Inventory of the Ancient Monuments Volume I and II
　　[Edinburgh] **1963**

Statistical Account of Scotland Vol IX 1791-1799.
　　[Reissued EP Publishing. Wakefield, England]

New Statistical Account of Scotland. Vol VIII
　　[Edinburgh and London] **1845**

Third Statistical Account of Scotland. Vol XVIII
　　[Glasgow] **1966**

Stirling Journal and Advertiser

Stirling Observer

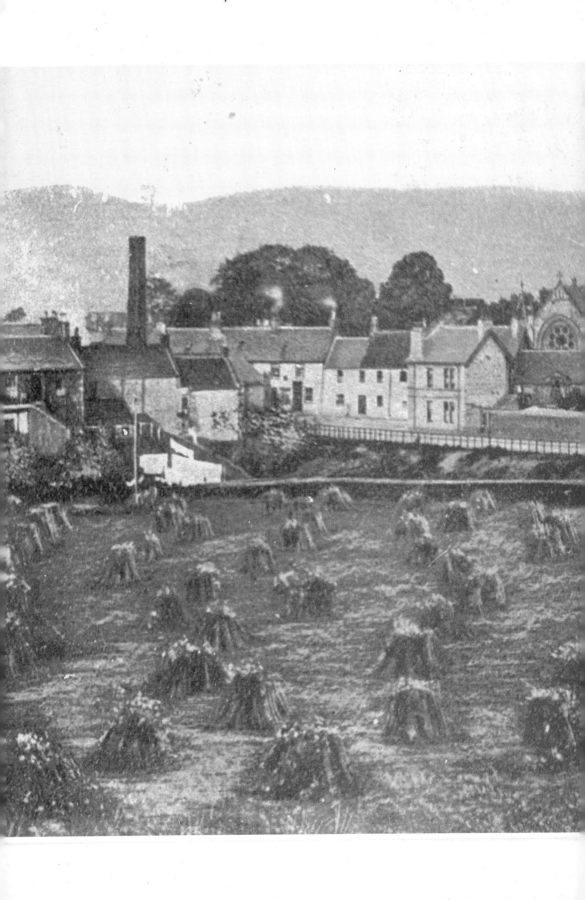